THE SOUL OF
MAN

The Soul Of Man. Copyright © 2021. C. Orville McLeish. All Rights Reserved.

No rights claimed for public domain material, all rights reserved. No parts of this publication may be reproduced, stored in any retrieval system, or transmitted in any form or by any means, electronic, mechanical, recording, or otherwise, without the prior written permission of the author. Violations may be subject to civil or criminal penalties.

ISBN: 978-1-953759-28-3 (paperback)
       978-1-953759-29-0 (eBook)

Scripture quotations marked "NKJV" are taken from the New King James Version. Copyright © 1982 by Thomas Nelson, Inc. Used by permission. All rights reserved. Bible text from the New King James Version® is not to be reproduced in copies or otherwise by any means except as permitted in writing by Thomas Nelson, Inc., Attn: Bible Rights and Permissions, P.O. Box 141000, Nashville, TN 37214-1000.

Scripture quotations marked "NASB" are taken from the New American Standard Bible®, Copyright © 1960, 1962, 1963, 1968, 1971, 1972, 1973, 1975, 1977, 1995 by The Lockman Foundation. Used by permission.

Scripture quotations marked "ESV" are from the ESV Bible® (The Holy Bible, English Standard Version®), copyright © 2001 by Crossway Bibles, a publishing ministry of Good News Publishers. Used by permission. All rights reserved.

Scripture quotations marked CSB have been taken from the Christian Standard Bible®, Copyright © 2017 by Holman Bible Publishers. Used by permission. Christian Standard Bible® and CSB® are federally registered trademarks of Holman Bible Publishers.

All Scripture quotations are taken from THE MESSAGE, copyright © 1993, 2002, 2018 by Eugene H. Peterson. Used by permission of NavPress. All rights reserved. Represented by Tyndale House Publishers, Inc.

Scripture quotations marked (CEV) are from the Contemporary English Version Copyright © 1991, 1992, 1995 by American Bible Society. Used by Permission.

Printed in the United States of America

THE SOUL OF MAN

Traversing the Mystery of Man As A Living Soul

C. Orville McLeish

I want to dedicate this book to my *son*, Ethan Johnson.

You were very young when I wrote and published this book, but when I became discouraged from thoughts of a lack of support and engagement from my generation, I think of you and how, just maybe, my words will make enough difference in your life to cause you to rise up to your fullest potential and fulfill the mandate you have to change the world and help usher in the emergence of a new heaven and a new earth.

Ethan, to you and your generation, leave this world better than how you found it.

Visit:

www.corvillemcleish.com

for more books and content that will help you on your faith journey.

To those whose sole desire is to become a full manifestation of God's intent when He said, "Let Us make man in Our image and likeness…"

Visit our youtube page @ God's Image Jamaica ([God's Image Jamaica - YouTube](#))

Let us change the world one maturing soul at a time!

TABLE OF CONTENTS

Introduction ___ *15*

Chapter One: The Soul of the Unbeliever ___ *23*

    Process of Salvation ___ 28

Chapter Two: Emergence of the Living Soul ___ *33*

Chapter Three: The Structures of the Soul ___ *43*

Chapter Four: The Garments of the Soul ___ *51*

Chapter Five: Maturing the Soul ___ *63*

    Once Enlightened ___ 67

    Tasted of the Heavenly Gift ___ 71

    Partakers of the Holy Ghost ___ 71

    Tasted of the Good Word of God ___ 72

    Powers of the World to Come ___ 76

Chapter Six: The Functionality of a Living Soul ___ *83*

Conclusion ___ *91*

    You Have Less Interest in Approval ___ 92

You Process Issues Faster	92
The Ego Is Replaced by Equanimity	93
Deepening and Abiding Sense of Love	93
You Are Drawn Towards Nourishment	94
You Are At Ease in Letting Go	95
You Appreciate the Human Process	96
Dear Younger Soul	*101*
Additional Text On The Soul	*121*
Quotes for the Maturing Soul	*145*

INTRODUCTION

Rabbi Dr. Aryeh Leibowitz, in his article titled: "Your Divine Soul: An Introduction," writes:

The Torah relates that mankind acquired a soul – a neshamah – when God "breathed" it into him at creation.

"And God formed man from the dust of the ground, and He breathed into his nostrils the soul of life, and man became a living soul (Genesis 2:7)."

Why does the Torah use this peculiar imagery of breathing to describe God's granting to man a soul?

The Soul of Man

Our Sages explain: "One who breathes, breathes from within himself."[1] Breathing requires one to exhale air from deep within themselves. When the Torah states that God "breathed" a soul into man, it teaches us that God gave over to man something of Him, so to speak. The breath of God imparted to man a spiritual, transcendent, and even God-like essence.

The abstract idea of a divine element existing within man is hard to understand in concrete terms. Therefore, our sages utilize borrowed terms – such as divine "light" or "energy" – when referring to this divine element in man. When the divinity of man's soul is actualized, illuminating an individual with divine light, man is referred to as "holy" or "sanctified" (Kadosh). Holiness exists when the divine is revealed in a physical entity.

---

[1] *Sefer Ha-Peliah* s.v., See also Ramban's commentary on Bereishis 2:7; R. Moshe Cordevero's *Shiur Komah*, chap. 51; and *Likutei Amarim Tanya*, chap. 2.

It is amazing that up until this day, only within the Jewish community and cultures is the relevance and value of a soul discussed. In the western world, the soul is frowned upon as being bad. We have developed a language that talks about man's "soulish" nature as being that which should be denied and suppressed. There are "soulish" music and ministers who operate from their "souls," and within all these references, the "soul" becomes a bad thing. Frankly, we have been completely misinformed as it relates to the soul.

The soul of man is the receptacle of the divine. Essentially, the soul is God, not in the sense that it *is* God, but it is the very essence and substance of the being of God. It is God multiplying Himself across the face of the earth, and by extension, across the created world. Every human being has a divine "God-spark" in them that truly comes to life when one accepts that they were made by Him and for Him. Otherwise, that divine spark remains uninitiated or, in lay man's terms, dead. It is not dead in the sense that it ceases to exist, but death in the sense that there is an absence of life or light.

The soul of man can be alive, or it can be devoid of life. The Rabbi continued to say:

> *The amount of divine light that can enter man and reside within him is dependent upon man himself. When man begins life, he has a greater identification with his physical being and is, by nature, a foreigner to holiness. Therefore, only a very small amount of divinity can initially enter and reside within him. But through great human effort, man is able (to) elevate himself and upgrade his inner receptacle for divinity.*

While it can be argued that man has one soul, which essentially is an unraveling mystery for us in this time, may I be permitted to complicate the matter even further to say that man has more than one soul. It may have been singular in the beginning, but by virtue of the fall, this is seemingly no longer the case, though one of the goals of redemption is for man to become whole again.

Here is a quote from Rabbi Dovid Rosenfeld:

> *Likewise, a man's soul consists of three parts. The lowest part is the breath which has come to rest in the person, known as his nefesh. It is basically the life-force which man shares with the entire animal kingdom. The human nefesh is understandably smarter and more competent, but it is a force not qualitatively*

different from that of any of God's creations. It controls the body's conscious and subconscious behavior and it responds to the physical stimuli it receives from the body.

The next stage moving up is man's ruach, usually translated as spirit. It corresponds to the "wind" which passes through the glassblower's tube. It is the first part of man's soul which is unique to mankind. As the blowing tube, it spans the universe, the infinite layers of reality spanning from the highest heavens to the physical world. Although it does not dwell within the body, being that it dwells right above it, it influences our bodies, sanctifying and connecting our nefesh within to the higher planes of existence. It serves as a conduit, connecting man's earthiest parts to his loftiest, bridging the gap between two realities which cannot possibly mix.

The loftiest part of man's soul is his neshama, literally the breath which has not left God Himself (if that could be stated). Man's neshama resides in the highest heavens; it emanates from a world higher than almost any other part of creation. It is far too lofty and

> *ethereal to have any direct connection with the physical world. It is man's pure soul, unsullied by any connection to physicality.* Yet, since man's Ruach connects it indirectly to man's body, one who is particularly worthy will have "sparks" of it emanate from above and influence him for the better. It is the part of us which gives us our deepest understanding of God and His Torah.

All this information is in the public archives, which means for there not to be any discussion of this subject across the western world, it can mean one of two things: either we are not searching for the information or do not believe this to be true.

In this book, I am beginning a discussion that may seem foreign to my generation and those before and beyond, especially here in the Western world, but it will resonate with those who will come after us because it is time for human beings to know who we are, and I do not believe God is holding anything back in releasing these revelations into the world.

As with all my other books, this is merely a summary --- a conversation starter, if you may, because having a conversation is the first step to spiritual transformation. The next step is to renew your mind with truth, which is by no means an easy process because one can get comfortable with what they already know and believe and lose interest in anything that contradicts that.

God is seemingly contradictory by nature because He will not give hard food to a baby, but He will allow you to think that milk is all there is where food is concerned.

Let us talk about man as a living soul, and may you find this conversation as equally enlightening as I did in researching, searching, learning, and putting the content together.

CHAPTER ONE
THE SOUL OF THE UNBELIEVER

It would be remiss to discuss man as a living soul without examining the soul of one who is not a believer. It is apparent from the very beginning of Scripture that those of us who are present in this "time bubble" was made in a certain light. We were meant to be a living soul, but we always had the power to choose a different path by virtue of free will.

The question has been asked for millennia, *"Why did God put the tree of the knowledge of good and evil in the garden if He knew we would eat from it?"* There are several layers to consider in answering this question. Firstly, Genesis documents a time when there was no veil and the physical and spiritual world operated as one. It would appear that God had a man to man conversation with Adam in the Garden, but God is Spirit, so it may not be what we think it is. Secondly, considering the first point, it was not just a tree that we are talking about. The keyword in that text is "knowledge." Good and evil was a knowledge the man and woman were not matured enough to partake of. Eating of any "fruit" before its time is detrimental, which is why some people believe and perpetuate a doctrine that the fall had to do with sex. There is a parallel that could be drawn between the two where early participation in such can be destructive and change the course of one's life.

So, back to the issue at hand. If God, who is the source of all life, determines to make human beings like Him, having a free will, God essentially created the possibility for evil by creating beings who could choose to reject Him. The tree of the knowledge of good and evil was not just put there in the Garden to tempt man; it was embedded in man at his creation. It was impossible for God to create man without creating the potential and possibility for both good and evil. God cannot clone Himself, so whatever He created must be lower than He is. Now, this does not negate man's value, for we are undoubtedly made in His image and likeness.

Lubavitcher Rebbe has a particular teaching that is of interest to scholars. His teaching was adapted by Moshe Yaakov Wisnefsky, and it says:

"God then formed man out of dust of the ground, and He blew into his nostrils a soul of life, and man became a living being." (Genesis 2:7)

"God then formed": *We do not find any mention of "creation" in this verse, for both the body and the soul were formed of pre-existing matter: the body from earth, and the soul from the essence of God.[2] Adam (and Eve) were created in the form of mature, twenty-year-old adults.[3]*

"And He breathed": *In contrast to the rest of Creation, which was created with God's speech, man's soul was given to him through God's breath. We all breathe constantly and can talk for hours on end. But after blowing for just a short time, a person becomes exhausted. This is because when blowing, the breath comes from deeper in the lungs than it does with simple breathing or talking. Thus, the idiom of God "breathing" man's soul into him*

---

[2] Sefer HaMa'amarim 5748, p. 14

[3] Bereishit Rabbah 14:7

indicates that man's soul originates from deeper "within" God than the rest of Creation. This simply means that man is the primary purpose of Creation while everything else is secondary and ancillary to him. Man's divine soul is a spark - i.e. a part of God. This soul can never lose its intrinsic connection with God. Man's challenge is to ensure that this connection remains manifested within his physical being. Just as when one blows, the air will only reach its destination if there are no obstructions, so can the Godly soul shine only if there are no obstacles that obscure it.[4]

By virtue of choice, man became a fallen being on the earth, which means that our original functionality and make up must have been affected. But man's value remains intact because if we measure the worth of something by what we are willing to pay for it, man's soul is of equal value to the life of God, who is sovereign. Still, humanity continues to make bad choices. Such a choice, to deviate from the ways of our Creator and the Sustainer of life, however, is not without consequences, as history has proven

---

[4] Tanya, ch. 2; Iggeret HaTeshuvah, ch. 4-5

repeatedly. The ramifications of disconnecting our will from that of our Creator have far-reaching, cosmic effects, resulting in our loss of identity and functionality. It would appear then that sin, which is essentially a derailment from the ways of God, is destructive to our souls.

If believers are given a new soul via salvation, then what does an unbeliever possess on the interior of his/her being? How can a believer also have an out of body experience? It is clear that non-believers practice astral projection as the fallen or counterfeit version of what a human being can do, but how is this possible if they have a dead soul?

It is clear that an unbeliever's soul is limited in its reach, but there is also a suggestion that a demonic entity is required for them not to lose their lives in the process. Prophetess Ana Mendez did a discourse that elaborated on a very mysterious verse of Scripture in the Bible:

Remember your Creator before the silver cord is loosed, Or the golden bowl is broken, Or the pitcher shattered at the fountain, Or the wheel broken at the well. (Ecclesiastes 12:6 - NKJV).

She said the silver cord is what keeps the body joined to the soul. The believer does not have a silver cord because Jesus has removed the concept of death, but it is still intact in an unbeliever. The Christian mystics will tell you that if an unbeliever astral projects and come into your presence, if you are mature enough, you can sever their silver cord and they will die.

I think one obvious contrast between a living and a dead soul is the light it carries. Believers are the light of the world. The new soul was hewn from the very fabric of God's being, and He is light. I imagine a dead soul would have a blank, cold, and gray appearance, though it is the soul of the one to whom it belongs.

Whatever flows from the dead soul will have the seed of death embedded in it, for example, medications, surgical procedures, and food. Whatever flows from the new living soul will be embedded with life.

Process of Salvation

Salvation is essentially a restoration of original intent and a revelation of humanity's true identity. Why was man created initially? I like Moshe Yaakov Wisnefsky's take on it:

God created man (in the fashion he was created) for two reasons:

Firstly, if an entity is to ascend, even its lowest part must ascend with it. Similarly, in order for man to fulfill his destiny of spiritually completing and perfecting the world, he must possess a bond with every aspect of Creation. Therefore, man's body was formed of the lowest common denominator so that even the lowest elements on the spiritual hierarchy can be rectified through him.[5] This gives us additional insight into Rashi's statement that God collected earth from all over the world to create man's body. By doing this, God made man encompass the entire material world he was to elevate.

Secondly, humankind's mission is to combine two opposites: the spiritual consciousness of Godliness with the darkness of the physical world. By creating man through a similar

---

[5] Torah Ohr, p. 7. Sefer HaMa'amarim 5714, pp. 126-7

> *fusion of extremes, God infused him with the natural capacity to do this.*[6]

Jesus made a profound statement: "I have come to make all things new" (Revelation 21:5). Jesus died to save our souls. From many Old Testament Scripture, we see that the atonement for sin by blood has to do with the soul. King David and Solomon placed great emphasis on the soul, so the conclusion is that Paul's exhortation about becoming a new creation in Christ must be focused primarily on the soul.

Accepting Jesus as Lord and Saviour initiates a divine process in heaven where a new soul is hewn from God's very being, and it passes through the matrix of time and eternity and infuses into the new believer. There must then be a shattering of the old dead soul, but is it completely removed? The reality of our struggles and fight with the flesh would suggest that at least the memory of sin remains in our body. Paul asked a very profound question: who will deliver him from the body of death (See Romans 7:24). Was he referring to his physical body or his soul body?

---

[6] Hitva'aduyot 5750, vol. 1, p.301; Sefer HaMa'amarim 5721,pp. 343-4)

Please take note that many different words with different connotations were translated as simply "body" in the English Bible. It takes a committed scholar to unearth the truth about the use of "body" in Scripture. In summary, a believer has access to many bodies, and not just one. We are not dealing with that in this book, so let us get back to the soul.

The good news is that God has provided a new soul that can influence, or to say it even better, bring redemption to all the other fallen aspects of our being because the new soul has direct access to God.

Salvation is God being born inside each believer in Christ. It is the same fundamental principle we see at work in the beginning when God breathes upon Adam, and he became a living soul. God now breathes upon the believer, and there is a divine transfer that shifts a human being from death to life.

The goal of the new soul is to bring rectification to the whole man, and then, by extension, to all creation. The Hebrew word for this new soul is "Yekidah" which becomes our window towards unity, towards union with God.

The unbeliever has a soul, but it is devoid of life. The believer is given a new soul, hewn from the fabric of

God's being, and so begins the rectification process that essentially moves us from death to life through the matrix of spiritual transformation.

CHAPTER TWO
EMERGENCE OF THE LIVING SOUL

The triune nature of man (spirit, soul, body), created in God's image and likeness, is one of the greatest mysteries of all time for the church. There have been significant medical and scientific discoveries as it relates to the body of man. Yet, there is no one expert who will claim he or she has even begun to understand its makeup and functionality. How much more is understanding man's spirit and soul, which extends beyond physicality, all the way back to eternity.

This book, by no means, seeks to present arguments from a position of authority and know-it-all, but it is written to help initiate a conversation on a very vital aspect of a man's being: the soul.

The first mention of the soul we see is in Genesis:

The Soul of Man

And the LORD God formed man *of* the dust of the ground, and breathed into his nostrils the breath of life; and man became a living soul. (Genesis 2:7)

Other translations replace the word "soul" with "being, creature, person," but most translations retain the word "soul." The original text used is the Hebrew word "nephesh."

*neh'-fesh: f*rom H5314; properly a *breathing* creature, that is, *animal* or (abstractly) *vitality*; used very widely in a literal, accommodated or figurative sense (bodily or mental): - any, appetite, beast, body, breath, creature, X dead (-ly), desire, X [dis-] contented, X fish, ghost, + greedy, he, heart (-y), (hath, X jeopardy of) life (X in jeopardy), lust, man, me, mind, mortality, one, own, person, pleasure, (her-, him-, my-, thy-) self, them (your) -selves, + slay, soul, + tablet, they, thing, (X she) will, X would have it.

The suggestion here is that humanity should have always paid attention to the idea of a "soul" being man and not man just as a body. While I believe in the value of the body because God made it, I believe the soul carries equal significance because Jesus came to save our souls.

Human beings were made in the image and likeness of God, and then something terrible happened that had a cosmic effect on creation: man fell, and sin and death were introduced into the context of man. It is also believed that men changed in appearance and functionality, for now, we see man hiding from God instead of being in communion with God. There was a "nakedness" that became apparent because what was original now looked different. Salvation will force us to revisit the idea of "original intent" repeatedly. If sin is the problem, then we want to know what life was like before sin.

There are many schools of thought as it relates to what happened that man was now naked and ashamed. There is no indication that they were wearing clothes in the first place. Some believe that man was covered with a celestial body, or the glory of God, so his nakedness was not exposed. The theory I am leaning towards is that man's soul was on the outside; as a literal covering for the body. As we proceed, and you see the structure and functionality of the soul and its ability to expand and travel to any place in time, outside of time, and in parts of creation that you are able to see in your imagination, it will become clear.

The Soul of Man

For centuries the church taught that man died a spiritual death in the Garden, but the truth may have been staring us dead in the eyes all this time, for it was the prophet Ezekiel who said:

Behold, all souls are mine; the soul of the father as well as the soul of the son is mine: the soul who sins shall die. (Ezekiel 18:4 – ESV).

What if this fall caused men's soul not just to die, but to be fragmented? What would that look like? How can we put the pieces back together? How do we get back to that place of original intent in appearance and functionality? It makes sense that Jesus would say on several occasions: "Be made whole." There must be some form of fragmentation for there to be a need for wholeness.

We do not know what human beings looked like or what they could do before the fall. The closest demonstration of this we see in human history is within that era when Divinity became a human being; when the Word became flesh and dwelt among us; when God became man, Jesus Christ. And even with all the knowledge that we Gentiles have of this "Man," we still have no idea how He functioned as a man because most of what was written is interpreted in a natural sense, and not a spiritual/mystical context.

Jesus, as a human being, is Adam before the fall, though there is a suggestion that He is greater.

So also it is written, "The first MAN, Adam, BECAME A LIVING SOUL." The last Adam became a life-giving spirit. (1 Corinthians 15:45 - NKJV).

Jesus, as a life-giving Spirit, is able to infuse life back into the soul, making man once again a "living soul." There is not much teaching, if any, among us as Gentiles on the soul of man. The soul before the fall was a life-giver; the soul after the fall was a death-carrier. Here is a theory to consider: Man was/is God's world.

For God so loved the world that He gave His only begotten Son, that whoever believes in Him should not perish but have everlasting life. (John 3:16 - NKJV).

Original man was the carrier of the world that God created. When man fell, there was a fragmentation that resulted in limitations where now there was a need for another "world" to emerge from fallen man for man to function. Everything we created to function in this world was as a result of the fall. This means that pre-fall functionality included being able to do what the plane, cars, cell phones, space shuttles, etc. is able to do. This means that the soul is expandable, able to communicate beyond spoken language, travel through multi-dimensions, etc. This, of course, is somewhat speculative, though it makes sense.

In order to grasp the spiritual reality of which I speak, it becomes necessary for us to first see the physical attributes that appeal to our physical sight as merely an illusion. Not an illusion in that it is non-existent, but an illusion in that it is merely a reflection of something more real in the real world (spiritual world). The disparity we see between the Biblical narrative and our own lives is because there is a lack of understanding and knowledge about the real world of which we are a part. The Bible does describe it in detail for us, but we opt to believe in what we can see as our reality, thereby losing consciousness with how the spiritual engages with us daily. We do not know when an angel is in our midst. We do not know when God is speaking to us. Most human beings do not even know the reason they came to earth. Yes, I believe we had a pre-existence in spiritual form before coming here. I also believe we choose to come here for a specific purpose, but that is not what we are talking about now.

The soul becomes our connection to the divine; to a heavenly, spiritual reality. The difference between us today and the characters from the Biblical era is that they understood their souls' functionality. They understood that the soul is *God*, connecting to God as a restorative principle that pulls us back to original intent. A lack of understanding of the soul, even and especially as a believer, can result in us being cut off from divine realities; we hear nothing, we see nothing; therefore, our walk becomes one of faith seeking evidence, or no faith at all.

If we cannot find the answers we seek about the soul in the culture, teachings and beliefs of the Gentile community, then it behoves us to look for this knowledge elsewhere; particularly in the community from which the Biblical narrative emerged: in the Jewish community. After all, Jesus was a Jew. He came as a Jew, out of the lineage of the Israelite community, who the Bible refers to as God's firstborn son. If the idea of salvation is rooted in the cultural norms of this community, then understanding Scripture and truth must come from that perspective as well.

There is a remarkable scripture that has baffled religious minds for centuries:

The Soul of Man

Therefore if any man be in Christ, he is a new creature: old things are passed away; behold, all things are become new. (2 Corinthians 5:17 – KJV).

If man is indeed a new creature by virtue of salvation, then why do we still struggle with the sin nature lodged within our beings? Why are so many Christians, even among the clergy, so adept to sin and addictions? The Word of God cannot lie, so what is new, and why is the old stuff still there?

We now go back to the statement of a fragmented soul. If a man had the functionality of self-duplication, then it is not too far-fetched to imagine that he is intrinsically made up of layers of souls, and not just one soul in the sense of what we know as singular. A new soul is given to the man who receives Christ as Lord and Saviour, but still, the possibility remains that there are other levels or dimensions of self that this new soul must influence in order for a man to become whole and, inevitably, transfigured. That is the ultimate goal of Christianity, is it not? For us to become Christ, so Christ can hand all things back over to the Father, who will inevitably become all in all.

Then, when all things are under his authority, the Son will put himself under God's authority, so that God, who gave his Son authority over all things, will be utterly supreme over everything everywhere. (1 Corinthians 15:28 - NLT).

I assume that God was utterly supreme over everything everywhere at some point before creating man. If I should push this thought to the limit, I would say that when man fell, we caused a part of God to become fragmented within creation, which is why salvation becomes so important to God. It is not just redeeming man as a fallen being, but redeeming His Son, who is the culmination of all humanity reconciled in one being that was once fallen, fragmented and scattered, and is now brought back whole and redeemed.

Adam was the embodiment of all humanity, as was Jesus Christ, which means that all humanity collectively is God's son and salvation is about bringing the fragmented body of the son back together again.

Take a small breather because this is a lot to digest.

Immortality becomes embedded in the human being because the soul is immortal. The believer who now becomes a living soul by virtue of the life-giving Spirit, who is Christ, must pass through the process of becoming the expressed image of God. This process extends beyond one's physical death because the epicenter of such activities is taking place with man as a soul.

CHAPTER THREE
THE STRUCTURES OF THE SOUL

The process of spiritual growth is intrinsically connected to our capacity to know ourselves. "Know thyself" is not a metaphor but a prerequisite to being able to recognize how God engages with us on a daily basis. It all begins with knowing ourselves. We must understand our particular strengths and weaknesses. From that vantage point, certainly, we are enjoined to avoid extremism and to ease ourselves towards the center. But our journey must begin with self-knowledge. For only when we know whom we are today can we begin the journey towards true fulfillment.[7]

There is a process that we must go through from the moment we are born from above (born again) as a "baby" soul, to growing up to maturity as a son of

---

[7] https://torah.org/learning/mlife-ch1law1/

God. Our Father takes responsibility for initiating and guiding that process, which suggests that most of us have not matured because we defeat and resist the process out of ignorance. If we do not know ourselves in terms of structure and functionality, particularly where our soul is concerned, then how are we to know God?

Knowing yourself incorporates knowing how every aspect of your being functions. You must know your emotions, thought processes, the core of your belief systems, your imagination, how nature and people, particularly language, affects you in your mind and body, etc. We are complex and multi-layered beings because, of course, God's image is still resident in us, though a bit distorted. In knowing ourselves, we learn how to change ourselves, where necessary, or at the very least, be able to identify when we are changing and when there is a need to change.

We change when we get saved. We get a new soul. That is the start of the redemptive process of our entire being because all that we are, known and unknown, must come in alignment with the new nature that we have received. Along with the new soul we are given all things pertaining to life and godliness and the mind of Christ. We are also given the Ruach

Hackodosh (Holy Spirit), who occupies our internal structure, as well as sits on our bodies. Remember, the goal is wholeness and transfiguration --- transcendence, if you are comfortable with that term.

In this chapter, I will be repeating some terms and phrases used by my mentor, who is the only one I have heard teach on the soul. As a matter of fact, everything I know about the soul, in addition to my own personal revelations that come from listening to him teach and scrolling through the over 400 references to the soul in Scripture is because of him. This entire book came out of the many hours of his teachings and deep contemplation of relevant Scriptural references. I will highlight his words in italics.

The new soul carries redemptive power for all the other souls in the body. What other souls, you may ask. Good question. In answering this, we must be mindful that we had a structure before we got saved. If there is something new at the moment of conversion, then what happened to the old? What was there before? Salvation does not change the body, which means the process must be internal. Thereby, we must pay attention to our internal structure because transfiguration happens from the inside out. So let us examine "self" internally.

The mind is usually associated with the soul. From Scripture, we know there is a mind in the heart and a mind in the head. There is also present inside a believer the mind of Christ. This speaks to at least three souls. *The soul in the brain is the first recipient of the gospel. The soul in the brain takes ideas and makes them work in physical reality.*

The new soul (Yekidah) lands on the head and begins to influence the other souls. This is how we have the capacity to work out our own salvation with fear and trembling. It is this new soul that brings redemption to all the other fallen souls in our body. If this is too much for you, then think in this regard: the new soul infuses life into the dead soul. It activates the divine principles once embedded in our living soul that became dormant (dead) when man fell. Examining the dead soul from the perspective of fragmentation, we begin to see the different aspects of our being that "needs God," in a manner of speaking.

The fullness or wholeness of our soul gives us the capacity to function in every arena of creation. Remember our original mandate:

Then God said, "Let Us make man in Our image, according to Our likeness; let them have dominion over the fish of the sea, over the birds of the air, and over the cattle, over all the earth and over every creeping thing that creeps on the earth." So God created man in His own image; in the image of God He created him; male and female He created them. Then God blessed them, and God said to them, "Be fruitful and multiply; fill the earth and subdue it; have dominion over the fish of the sea, over the birds of the air, and over every living thing that moves on the earth." (Genesis 1:26-28 - NKJV).

On this side of life, we have no idea what replenish, rule, and dominion looked like until God spoke to Job. I will add these Scriptures under the *Function Of The Soul* chapter.

What are the different souls in the body?

This knowledge is still new to me, but an observation of self can reveal divine mysteries to the heart that is open to receive.

There is a soul in our brain. We can call this the intellectual soul, and this is the first point of contact as the Yekidah begins to flow down into the body. The heart is connected to this soul, thereby giving man his creative ability, for it is the *heart that gives the voice the power to create.*

There is the apparent animal nature. We see this playing out in our society by men and women who shun salvation. They act more like animals than humans. When we become a believer, this nature seems to remain, so let us call this the animal soul.

There is the vegetative soul, which acts as the inanimate aspect of the body. *When that son of God (new soul) permeates the entire being, the inorganic world responds to come to life again.*

For the earnest expectation of the creation eagerly waits for the revealing of the sons of God. For the creation was subjected to futility, not willingly, but because of Him who subjected it in hope; because the creation itself also will be delivered from the bondage of corruption into the glorious liberty of the children of God. (Romans 8:19-21 - NKJV).

The idea that creation is groaning for the manifestation of the sons of God suggests that the new soul must come into maturity or perfection. The Yekidah frames the Nephimah.

The soul of Adam was not inside Adam, but outside. Man was able to do far more than we can do now, yet the reality of the "original design" sits within the believer, though, in potential and restrained by ignorance. The soul is the real you. The very essence of your life is a combination of your body, the breath of God, and the soul. The soul can exist without the body, but the body cannot exist without the soul.

When you die, your consciousness remains with you. The memory seems optional because we do not recall most of what our souls engage in at nights while we sleep, but the issue we struggle with: our emotions, personality, characteristics, how we respond to people, our growth or lack thereof is all embedded in our soul and goes with us to the other side. This means the very issues we need to overcome now to come into manifestation as sons, follow us when we cross over from this world, and remains something we need to face and overcome.

The maturity of the soul then becomes mandatory, not optional.

CHAPTER FOUR
THE GARMENTS OF THE SOUL

In the same way the body needs garments for various reasons and functions, there are also garments for the soul. When you first begin to cloth yourself in the garments of the soul, they will feel like they fit big, but the soul was designed to grow into these garments. Wearing the wrong garments decreases the light and power of God embedded in the believer.

Here is an excerpt from my "Who AM I in Christ Prayer Journal":

> Have you ever put on a piece of clothing that was way too big for your size? ... as you continue to daily cloth yourselves in them, your soul has the capacity to grow into them. It is important that regardless of how you feel or how negatively you see yourself, that you daily cloth your soul with

The Soul of Man

(the garments God provides) ... for it speaks to who you are.

These garments relating to your identity was made specifically for you. They do not fit perfectly now because you were not "born again" as an adult; you came out of the water and Spirit as a baby in Christ. The problem with Christianity is that it is easy to get stuck in infancy, but that was not the original intention for you. As a babe, you are naked and unashamed, but as you grow older, the need arises for you to be clothed. The environment in which we grow tend to put on their own garments to cover up our nakedness, but they are not the garments we were intended to wear. Thereby, in putting on the real garments of the soul, we must put off the temporary, debilitating ones.

Paul alludes to the putting off and putting on of the garments of the soul more than any other Biblical writer:

For as many of you as were baptized into Christ have put on Christ. (Galatians 3:27).

But put on the Lord Jesus Christ, and make no provision for the flesh, to fulfill its lusts. (Romans 13:14).

And have put on the new man who is renewed in knowledge according to the image of Him who created him. (Colossians 3:10).

And that you put on the new man which was created according to God, in true righteousness and holiness. (Ephesians 4:24).

The night is far spent, the day is at hand. Therefore let us cast off the works of darkness, and let us put on the armor of light. (Romans 13:12).

Put on the whole armor of God, that you may be able to stand against the wiles of the devil. Stand therefore, having girded your waist with truth, having put on the breastplate of righteousness. (Ephesians 6:11,14).

But let us who are of the day be sober, putting on the breastplate of faith and love, and as a helmet the hope of salvation. (1 Thessalonians 5:8).

Therefore, as the elect of God, holy and beloved, put on tender mercies, kindness, humility, meekness, longsuffering. (Colossians 3:12).

But above all these things put on love, which is the bond of perfection. (Colossians 3:14).

For in this we groan, earnestly desiring to be clothed with our habitation which is from heaven, if indeed, having been clothed, we shall not be found naked. For we who are in this tent groan, being burdened, not because we want to be unclothed, but further clothed, that mortality may be swallowed up by life. (2 Corinthians 5:2-4).

Do not lie to one another, since you have put off the old man with his deeds. (Colossians 3:9).

That you put off, concerning your former conduct, the old man which grows corrupt according to the deceitful lusts. (Ephesians 4:22).

Therefore, putting away lying, "Let each one of you speak truth with his neighbor," for we are members of one another. (Ephesians 4:25).

The night is far spent, the day is at hand. Therefore let us cast off the works of darkness, and let us put on the armor of light. (Romans 13:12).

Therefore we also, since we are surrounded by so great a cloud of witnesses, let us lay aside every weight, and the sin which so easily ensnares us, and let us run with endurance the race that is set before us. (Hebrews 12:1).

Therefore lay aside all filthiness and overflow of wickedness, and receive with meekness the implanted word, which is able to save your souls. (James 1:21).

Therefore, laying aside all malice, all deceit, hypocrisy, envy, and all evil speaking. (1 Peter 2:1).

Do an honest assessment of yourself; what are you wearing that you need to put off, and what are you not wearing that you need to put on? Self-assessment is a necessary practice to know what you are wearing. Unless the soul is wearing its proper garments, it cannot engage in the rectification of the whole being.

How does the new soul begin to remedy the old souls? It is done through clothing the other souls with garments provided by God for the rectifying of a man's being. We see these garments in Scripture, but we interpreted them from a perspective of "work" and "effort" and not from receiving and putting on. It is believed that there are some forty garments that we need to be clothed in. This equates to passing through forty dimensions for the transmutation of the human being back to godhood. What is amazing is that most of the characters, if not all, that we admire in Scripture and seek to emulate have passed through the forty dimensions/levels of clothing the souls within themselves and coming into maturity.

Next the Messenger-Angel showed me the high priest Joshua. He was standing before God's Angel where the Accuser showed up to accuse him. Then God said to the Accuser, "I, God, rebuke you, Accuser! I rebuke you and choose Jerusalem. Surprise! Everything is going up in flames, but I reach in and pull out Jerusalem!" Joshua, standing before the angel, was dressed in dirty clothes. The angel spoke to his attendants, "Get him out of those filthy clothes," and then said to Joshua, "Look, I've stripped you of your sin and dressed you up in clean clothes." (Zechariah 3:1-4 - MSG).

It is God Himself who strips us of sin and provides the new garments that we wear. So now Paul says:

Assuming that you have heard about him and were taught in him, as the truth is in Jesus, to put off your old self, which belongs to your former manner of life and is corrupt through deceitful desires, and to be renewed in the spirit of your minds, and to put on the new self, created after the likeness of God in true righteousness and holiness. (Ephesians 4:21-24).

So there is a putting off and a putting on in the process of transmutation. Salvation is provided freely, at the cost of God's life, but it must be worked out in the life of the believer. Those who expect an automated process will get stuck in the birthing chamber and never emerge as a greater version of themselves. They will die and carry their immaturity into the other world, where they still need to go through the process.

After we begin to cloth ourselves in the newness of life, God gives us a responsibility that comes with added benefits:

God's Angel then charged Joshua, "Orders from God-of-the-Angel-Armies: 'If you live the way I tell you and remain obedient in my service, then you'll make the decisions around here and oversee

my affairs. And all my attendants standing here will be at your service.'" (Zechariah 3:6-7).

What creation is groaning for is for the fully matured son, as in the body of Christ; one body. So while it is good that one person achieves transcendence, and manifest as Moses, Elijah, David, Solomon did, there is a greater call for the body of Christ to grow up into the head (who is Christ), and it is when this body is matured, and transfigured that we will see creation rising up to become, once again, what it had been initially.

There are at least forty garments of the soul, and we see the concept of "forty" repeated several times in Scripture. Moses was 40 when he left Egypt, 80 when he had the burning bush experience, and 120 when he "died." We see him go "up into the mountain" for 40 days twice. Elijah fasted for 40 days. Jesus fasted for 40 days before coming out in the full power of the Holy Spirit. He also spent 40 days with His disciples after He rose from the dead, before His final ascension. There were 120 days before the day of Pentecost. Do you see?

Let us briefly look at a few of these garments. There is a garment of fire, which is elemental. Other elementals are earth, air, and water. The heart carries its own garment, which is the love of God and the fear of heaven and must be clothed appropriately to function effectively.

There are celestial, terrestrial, etc., garments. Here we see some of the garments made available for the soul:

There are also celestial bodies and terrestrial bodies; but the glory of the celestial is one, and the glory of the terrestrial is another. There is one glory of the sun, another glory of the moon, and another glory of the stars; for one star differs from another star in glory. So also is the resurrection of the dead. The body is sown in corruption, it is raised in incorruption. It is sown in dishonor, it is raised in glory. It is sown in weakness, it is raised in power. It is sown a natural body, it is raised a spiritual body. There is a natural body, and there is a spiritual body. And so it is written, "The first man Adam became a living being." The last Adam became a life-giving spirit. However, the spiritual is not first, but the natural, and afterward the spiritual. The first man was of the earth, made of dust; the second Man is the Lord from heaven. As was the man of dust, so also are those who are made of dust; and as is the heavenly Man, so also are those who are heavenly. And as we have borne

the image of the man of dust, we shall also bear the image of the heavenly Man. Now this I say, brethren, that flesh and blood cannot inherit the kingdom of God; nor does corruption inherit incorruption. Behold, I tell you a mystery: We shall not all sleep, but we shall all be changed— in a moment, in the twinkling of an eye, at the last trumpet. For the trumpet will sound, and the dead will be raised incorruptible, and we shall be changed. For this corruptible must put on incorruption, and this mortal must put on immortality. (1 Corinthians 15:40-53 - NKJV).

Can you extract all the garments that are embedded in this text? Give it a try!

Our soul carries a more divine and expandable intellect than our natural intellect, which is why we can keep learning no matter how old we get. The process of growth is always tied to learning, which puts greater responsibilities on teachers, which is why teachers are held at a higher regard than all the other gifts.

A teacher must possess the ability to shift a soul intellectually by always teaching above the level at which the soul presently is. This is what we do in schools but are afraid to do in church. While this is not a comprehensive and detailed study regarding the garments of the soul, it is enough to provoke further study, and contemplation so God can continue to unravel the mystery of these garments for us. The end game is the maturation of the soul.

CHAPTER FIVE
MATURING THE SOUL

The book of Hebrews chapters 5 and 6 has a profound discourse on the process of salvation that leads us into maturity as sons of God.

For though by this time you ought to be teachers, you need someone to teach you again the first principles of the oracles of God; and you have come to need milk and not solid food. For everyone who partakes only of milk is unskilled in the word of righteousness, for he is a babe. But solid food belongs to those who are of full age, that is, those who by reason of use have their senses exercised to discern both good and evil. Therefore, leaving the discussion of the elementary principles of Christ, let us go on to perfection, not laying again the foundation of repentance from dead works and of faith toward God, of the doctrine of baptisms, of laying on of hands, of resurrection of the dead, and of eternal judgment. And this we will do if God

permits. For it is impossible for those who were once enlightened, and have tasted the heavenly gift, and have become partakers of the Holy Spirit, and have tasted the good word of God and the powers of the age to come, if they fall away, to renew them again to repentance, since they crucify again for themselves the Son of God, and put Him to an open shame. (Hebrews 5:12-14 - 6:1-6 - NKJV).

The author of Hebrews addresses both perception and language. Spiritual and intellectual growth is always intrinsically related to speech and thought. In order to shift dimensions, we must start to think different thoughts, which influences a change in our language. Here the author advises that we move away from just discussing the elementary principles of Christ that we were taught and move on to other things; we do this first by changing our language. The last listing is of great interest to me because it speaks to levels of maturity for the soul:

1. Enlightenment

2. Taste the heavenly gift

3. Become partakers of the Holy Spirit

4. Tasted of the Good Word of God

5. Tasted of the powers of the age to come

These terms are not in the everyday "church" language. It is the language of sons as we engage on the ancient paths of maturing our souls. This level is referred to as coming into perfection or maturity. It is first a language; a thought process, before it becomes a living reality. Paul says in Romans 8:22-25: *"All around us we observe a pregnant creation. The difficult times of pain throughout the world are simply birth pangs. But it's not only around us; it's within us. The Spirit of God is arousing us within. We're also feeling the birth pangs. These sterile and barren bodies of ours are yearning for full deliverance. That is why waiting does not diminish us, any more than waiting diminishes a pregnant mother. We are enlarged in the waiting. We, of course, don't see what is enlarging us. But the longer we wait, the larger we become, and the more joyful our expectancy." (MSG).*

There is a groaning emanating from the very heart of creation for sons of God to come into maturity. Note that creation is not waiting for the *acts* of the sons of God. It is not what we do but who we are that will rectify creation. It is the manifestation of the living soul that creation awaits. In layman's terms, the wait is for you to show up in the fullness of who you are. Creation has not functioned at its fullest capacity since the fall of man. While redemption is a reality in the earth, the immaturity of believers, who believe that only physical death can bring us into the fullness of who we are, cause God's creation to exist in a lesser form than it was meant to. Jesus showed us what is possible because He walked in the fullness of what it means to be fully human on the earth. We thought He was just being God so we could go to heaven. Salvation has to do with redeeming all creation by first repositioning man in God, so man can do what he was created to do. We are the expressed image of God in creation, which means we are the reflection God sees if He should look in a mirror.

We must try to become mature and start thinking about more than just the basic things we were taught about Christ. (Hebrews 6:1 – CEV).

We are called to be partakers of God's divine nature, which means, as human beings, as believers, some measure of divinity exists in us as co-heirs, co-labourers, and co-inheritors of the kingdom of God. This divinity is the soul of man.

C. Orville McLeish

Once Enlightened

Enlightenment speaks to a spiritual awakening.

That's why, when I heard of the solid trust you have in the Master Jesus and your outpouring of love to all the followers of Jesus, I couldn't stop thanking God for you—every time I prayed, I'd think of you and give thanks. But I do more than thank. I ask—ask the God of our Master, Jesus Christ, the God of glory—to make you intelligent and discerning in knowing him personally, your eyes focused and clear, so that you can see exactly what it is he is calling you to do, grasp the immensity of this glorious way of life he has for his followers, oh, the utter extravagance of his work in us who trust him—endless energy, boundless strength! All this energy issues from Christ: God raised him from death and set him on a throne in deep heaven, in charge of running the universe, everything from galaxies to governments, no name and no power exempt from his rule. And not just for the time being, but forever. He is in charge of it all, has the final word on everything. At the center of all this, Christ rules the church. The church, you see, is not peripheral to the world; the world is peripheral to the church. The church is Christ's body, in which he speaks and acts, by which he fills everything with his presence. (Ephesians 1:15-23 - MSG).

Another translation says:

That the God of our Lord Jesus Christ, the Father of glory, may give to you the spirit of wisdom and revelation in the knowledge of Him, the eyes of your understanding being enlightened; that you may know what is the hope of His calling, what are the riches of the glory of His inheritance in the saints, and what is the exceeding greatness of His power toward us who believe, according to the working of His mighty power which He worked in Christ when He raised Him from the dead and seated Him at His right hand in the heavenly places, far above all principality and power and might and dominion, and every name that is named, not only in this age but also in that which is to come. (Ephesians 1:17-21 - NKJV).

This is not referring to the physical eyes, but the eyes of the soul; the eyes of the heart. There is an eye that needs to open for us to begin coming into maturity.

The lamp of the body is the eye. If therefore your eye is good, your whole body will be full of light.

But if your eye is bad, your whole body will be full of darkness. If therefore the light that is in you is darkness, how great is that darkness! (Matthew 6:22-23 - NKJV).

Enlightenment is defined as having or showing a rational, modern, and well-informed outlook. It has a lot to do with how we perceive reality—specifically, spiritual reality. If the fall made us unconscious of our spiritual reality, enlightenment makes us conscious.

We can see, and we should see, into the kingdom of God, whether our physical eyes are open or closed. One translation says, "…the eyes of the heart." I believe spiritual sight is tied to the pureness of the heart:

Blessed are the pure in heart, for they shall see God. (Matthew 5:8 - NKJV).

Let us unpack this before moving on. The heart is connected to speech/language:

A good man out of the good treasure of his heart brings forth good; and an evil man out of the evil treasure of his heart brings forth evil. For out of the abundance of the heart his mouth speaks. (Luke 6:45 - NKJV).

God has put eternity in the heart of the believer:

He has made everything beautiful in its time. Also He has put eternity in their hearts, except that no one can find out the work that God does from beginning to end. (Ecclesiastes 3:11 - NKJV).

Then King Solomon says:

Death and life are in the power of the tongue, and those who love it will eat its fruit. (Proverbs 18:21 - NKJV).

If the heart is the central housing for eternity, and the mouth speaks from the abundance of the heart, then the principle of life and death is intrinsically embedded in language, and there must a pureness of the heart for the eyes of the soul to see.

Also, our minds and imagination play a role in us seeing in the Spirit, so we need to know how to utilize what we have to access the spiritual realm.

The concept of knowing thyself plays a role here as well. Spiritual practices, such as worship, prayer, meditation, etc. all help with enlightenment, but as we approach these practices, the sole purpose of our hearts must be to know God, not to perform for others.

Tasted of the Heavenly Gift

The greatest gift humanity has ever received is God. It is the mystery of all ages. One Christian Mystic said it like this, "Jesus could have summed up His ministry by saying, 'I became man for you. If you don't become God for me, you dishonour me." (paraphrased).

Someone said, "Taste and see that the Lord is good." This speaks to intimacy—real intimacy, not intellectual intimacy.

Partakers of the Holy Ghost

"Partakers" suggest that we are called to be participants in whatever God is doing. It means playing an active role in whatever the Holy Ghost is doing. To partake of something is to participate or share in the fullness of that thing. Those who are partakers of the Holy Ghost share in His divine power. God shares His nature with us by joining Himself to us. We have access to the fullness of the God-head.

Let us look at a Biblical example:

And the Lord said to Moses, "Why do you cry to Me? Tell the children of Israel to go forward. But lift up your rod, and stretch out your hand over the sea and divide it. And the children of Israel shall go on dry ground through the midst of the sea." (Exodus 14:15-16 - NKJV).

The power to part the Red Sea was already inside Moses. He just needed the instruction. Those who are partakers of the Holy Spirit will first receive the instruction, then participate and then experience the manifestation.

The idea of being filled with the Holy Spirit as a believer is an enablement to do what God does. Every matured son of God will tell you they only do what they see the Father doing.

Then Jesus answered and said to them, "Most assuredly, I say to you, the Son can do nothing of Himself, but what He sees the Father do; for whatever He does, the Son also does in like manner." (John 5:19 - NKJV).

Tasted of the Good Word of God

For the word of God is living and active and sharper than any two-edged sword, and piercing as

far as the division of soul and spirit, of both joints and marrow, and able to judge the thoughts and intentions of the heart. (Hebrews 4:12 – NASB)

I think we do the "Word of God" a great injustice by limiting Him to only a book when He is so much more. Jesus is the Word who became flesh and dwelt among us (See John 1:14). There is no disputing this as fact:

God, after He spoke long ago to the fathers in the prophets in many portions and in many ways, in these last days has spoken to us in His Son, whom He appointed heir of all things, through whom also He made the world. (Hebrews 1:1-2 – NASB).

But there is something we may have missed in how we interpret the Scriptures because it was Jesus, the Word made flesh, who said:

It is written, 'Man shall not live on bread alone, but on every word that proceeds out of the mouth of God.' (Matthew 4:4 – NASB).

Jesus was quoting a Scripture from Deuteronomy, and this reference to the Word was not about the Bible. The Bible does not contain all the Words spoken by God, and every mention of the "Word of God" in

Scripture was written before there was a Bible. The correction here is not to idolize the Bible and make it God. We need to see the Bible's importance in its proper context.

In the beginning was the Word, and the Word was with God, and the Word was God. (John 1:1 – NASB)

This text speaks to three different levels of the Word converging into One Person. The Word of God is a spiritual entity in which we live, move, breathe and have our existence. The reality is, the world and everything in it is held together by the vibrational frequency of the voice of God, which means His voice reverberates throughout creation and holds everything together. If God stopped speaking for a milli-second, the world and everything in it would disappear and cease to exist. It is true that God is God all by Himself. It is only by His voice can anything else exist. If we wanted to really push this even further, we could say that when God made man, we became the voice of God in creation. We are a manifested word of God, which means that by our voice, we could very well be creating the world in which we live.

From a scientific perspective, the human body is made up of 37.2 trillion cells. If you pull these cells apart, the body will disappear because the cells are not visible to the human eye. What science cannot definitively say is what holds these cells together. I believe the answer is "the Word of God."

The Bible speaks of the Word of God as a living entity:

- ∂ the Word of God came to Nathan (See 1 Chronicles 17:3).

- ∂ the Word of God increased (See Acts 6:7).

- ∂ the Word of God grew and multiplied (See Acts 12:24).

- ∂ the Word of God grew mightily and prevailed (See Acts 19:20).

- ∂ the Word of God is quick, and powerful, and sharper than any two-edged sword (See Hebrews 4:12).

- ∂ the Word of God liveth and abideth forever (See 1 Peter 1:23).

- ∂ His name is called the Word of God (See Revelation 19:13).

The Word of God is tangible and can be seen. Proverbs 30:5 refers to the Word of God as "he." The Word of God is also referred to as a seed, which means it can produce something.

We are commissioned to eat the good Word of God and live an abundant life. This is more than just reading the Bible. God has always desired for us to encounter and experience Him. The Bible was written to help us know when it is Him that we are experiencing. There are other *beings* that come into the earth pretending to be God.

We must see the Word of God as more than just a book. We grossly limit God and ourselves by doing this.

Powers of the World to Come

But as it is written: **"Eye has not seen, nor ear heard, nor have entered into the heart of man the things which God has prepared for those who love Him." But God has revealed them to us through His Spirit. For the Spirit searches all things, yes, the deep things of God. (1 Corinthians 2:9-10 - NKJV).**

The Holy Spirit has access to everything that is hidden in God, and we have access to the Holy Spirit. We have the Holy Spirit; we have the mind of Christ.

The world to come is the world that existed before time was created. It is the realm outside of time, space and matter called eternity. Everything that God has for us in that realm was already ours before time, and we have access to it now.

Just as He chose us in Him before the foundation of the world, that we should be holy and without blame before Him in love. (Ephesians 1:4 - NKJV).

David partook of the Holy Spirit before the Holy Spirit was given:

Create in me a clean heart, O God, and renew a steadfast spirit within me. Do not cast me away from Your presence, and do not take Your Holy Spirit from me. (Psalm 51:10-11 - NKJV).

You will realize just how powerful that prayer was, because David understood the importance of maintaining a pure heart, and we do this by learning to control our thought process.

Casting down arguments and every high thing that exalts itself against the knowledge of God, bringing every thought into captivity to the obedience of Christ. (2 Corinthians 10: - NKJV).

As you mature as a son, you will begin to realize that Paul was referring to a constant internal conflict in this text. Our greatest battle for prominence and transcendence is always internal.

The powers of the world to come suggest that everything heaven has to offer us is available to us now. In order to access what is ours, we must learn to live from the "Now" and the "Lord's Day," and not from the seven days of the week (which is really paganistic in nature and function).

Here is an excerpt from one of my blog post at www.corvillemcleish.com:

> *In Genesis, there was the evening and the morning that constituted a day, even before the sun, moon, and stars came into existence. Even then, I am sure time did not progress as it does after the fall of man because everything changed when man fell. So, I am thinking that the Lord's Day either began in the beginning of time, or it began after His death, burial,*

ressurection and ascension. It is "His Day" and another word used in Scripture is "Now."

"Now faith is the substance of things hoped for, the evidence of things not seen." (Hebrews 11:1).

"For he saith, I have heard thee in a time accepted, and in the day of salvation have I succoured thee: behold, now is the accepted time; behold, now is the day of salvation." (2 Corinthians 6:2).

The Lord's Day is also the Last Day, not days. This day, which is called "now" is a perpetual day that is constituted by changes in era or ages, where one age ends, and another begins, but this day has an end when time as we know it will be no more. Some call it the restoration of all things; some say it is the consummation of the marriage between Jesus and His bride; I believe it is a glorious day when Jesus "...present the church to himself in spendor, without spot or wrinkle or anything like that, but holy and blameless." (Ephesians 5:27 – CSB).

The maturing soul needs the right environment to flourish and grow. The Bible refers to such an environment as liberty:

Now the Lord is the Spirit, and where the Spirit of the Lord is, there is liberty. (2 Corinthians 3:17 - NASB).

Leaders must understand this and create a nurturing environment for the one who is having spiritual/mystical experiences as the soul grows. There must be freedom for such a one to explore the depths of God and the realms of the kingdom.

Leaders must be caring, accomodating, provide guidance, and even Biblical correction, where necessary. Be mindful though, that Biblical correction does not mean the leader believes something, so everyone else must believe the same thing. The perspective and interpretation of scripture will be remarkably different for the one who experiences God in a mystical/spiritual way and the one who has no spiritual experiences.

In the kingdom of God, there is really no need for everyone to believe the same thing or the same way for there to be unity. What the body of Christ needs is unity in diversity. The interpretation of the world will be different for the toes than it is for the fingers. Both are correct. Doctrinal war and denominational conflict is merely a distraction. No one person or body of people has all the parts of God, yet every member is needed for the body to be matured.

For we know in part and we prophesy in part; but when the perfect comes, the partial will be done away. (1 Corinthians 13:9-10 - NASB).

CHAPTER SIX
THE FUNCTIONALITY OF A LIVING SOUL

How do we function as believers? Man was made with the capacity to do certain things. While there are snippets and insight into these responsibilities scattered throughout Scripture, there is one place that gives us a comprehensive listing that is worth personal and intentional study:

Then the Lord answered Job out of the whirlwind, and said: "Who is this who darkens counsel by words without knowledge? Now prepare yourself like a man; I will question you, and you shall answer Me. "Where were you when I laid the foundations of the earth? Tell Me, if you have understanding. Who determined its measurements? Surely you know! Or who stretched the line upon it? To what were its foundations fastened? Or who laid its cornerstone, when the morning stars sang together, and all the sons of God shouted for joy? "Or who shut in the sea with doors, when it burst forth and issued from the womb; when I made the clouds its garment, and thick darkness its swaddling band; when I fixed My limit for it, and set bars and doors; when I said, 'This far you may come, but no farther, and here your proud waves must stop!' "Have you commanded the morning since your days began, and caused the dawn to know its place, that it might take hold of the ends of the earth, and the wicked be shaken out of it? It takes on form like clay under a seal, and stands out like a garment. From the wicked their light is withheld, and the upraised arm is broken. "Have you entered the springs of the sea? Or have you walked in search of the depths? Have the gates of death been revealed to you? Or have you seen the doors of the shadow of death? Have you comprehended the breadth of the earth? Tell Me, if you know all this. "Where is the way to the dwelling of light? And darkness, where is its place, that you may take it to its territory, that you may know the paths to its home? Do you know it, because you were born then, or because the number of your days is great? "Have you entered the treasury of snow, or have you seen the treasury of hail, which I have reserved for the time of trouble, for the day of battle and war? By what way is light diffused, or the east wind scattered over the earth? "Who has divided a channel for the overflowing water, or a path for the thunderbolt, to cause it to rain on a land where there is no one, a wilderness in which there is no man; to satisfy the desolate waste, and cause to spring forth the growth of tender grass? Has the rain a father? Or who has begotten the drops of dew? From whose womb comes the ice? And the frost of heaven, who gives it birth? The waters harden like stone, and the surface of the deep is frozen. "Can you bind the cluster of the Pleiades, or loose the belt of Orion? Can you bring out Mazzaroth in its season? Or can you guide the Great Bear with its cubs? Do you know the ordinances of the heavens? Can you set their dominion over the earth? "Can you lift up your voice to the clouds, that an abundance of water may cover you? Can you send out lightnings, that they may go, and say to you, 'Here we are!'? Who has put wisdom in the mind? Or who has given understanding to the heart? Who can number the clouds by wisdom? Or who can pour out the bottles of heaven, when the dust hardens in clumps, and the clods cling together? "Can you hunt the prey for the lion, or satisfy the appetite of the young lions, when they crouch in their dens, or lurk in their lairs to lie in wait? Who provides food for the raven, when its young ones cry to God, and wander about for lack of food? "Do you know the time when the wild mountain goats bear young? Or can you mark when the deer gives birth? Can you number the months that they fulfill? Or do you know the time when they bear young? They bow down, they bring forth their young, they deliver their offspring. Their young ones are healthy, they grow strong with grain; they depart and do not return to them. "Who set the wild donkey free? Who loosed the bonds of the onager, whose home I have made the wilderness, and the barren land his dwelling? He scorns the tumult of the city; he does not heed the shouts of the driver. The range of the mountains is his pasture, and he searches after every green thing. "Will the wild ox be willing to serve you? Will he bed by your manger? Can you bind the wild ox in the furrow with ropes? Or will he plow the valleys behind you? Will you trust him because his strength is great? Or will you leave your labor to him? Will you trust him to bring home your grain, and gather it to your threshing floor? "The wings of the ostrich wave proudly, but are her wings and pinions like the kindly stork's? For she leaves her eggs on the ground, and warms them in the dust; she forgets that a foot may crush them, or that a wild beast may break them. She treats her young harshly, as though they were not hers; her labor is in vain, without concern, because God deprived her of wisdom, and did not endow her with understanding. When she lifts herself on high, she scorns the horse and its rider. "Have you given the horse strength? Have you clothed his neck with thunder? Can you frighten him like a locust? His majestic snorting strikes terror. He paws in the valley, and rejoices in his strength; he gallops into the clash of arms. He mocks at fear, and is not frightened; nor does he turn back from the sword. The quiver rattles against him, the glittering spear and javelin. He devours the distance with fierceness and rage; nor does he come to a halt because the trumpet has sounded. At the blast of the trumpet he says, 'Aha!' He smells the battle from afar, the thunder of captains and shouting. "Does the hawk fly by your wisdom, and spread its wings toward the south? Does the eagle mount up at your command, and make its nest on high? On the rock it dwells and resides, on the crag of the rock and the stronghold. From there it spies out the prey; its eyes observe from afar. Its young ones suck up blood; and where the slain are, there it is." (Job 38-39 - NKJV).

These two chapters in Job are very interesting. Initially, at first glance, it would appear these are things that God does that a man is incapable of doing. But if we examine the listing carefully, we see that this is what "rule and dominion and replenishing" would look like in the creation for man. It would appear that when man fell in the book of Genesis, he absolved his responsibilities in creation. The fall caused a cosmic change in man and how he was able to function in creation, so admittedly, man would have been unable to carry out the responsibilities given to him by virtue of creation. It means these things still needed to be done. If the reality is that God is presently doing these things, it is because man has still not ascended to the position of maturity in order to return to his full responsibility in creation. Again we see the relevance of this text:

For we know that the whole creation groans and labors with birth pangs together until now. (Romans 8:22 - NKJV).

From all indication, and on the merit of this book, though not at all exhaustive, there is much work to be done on ourselves. The good news is, we have a new soul, and we are born from above. We start there and must work through the process in order to come into wholeness or maturity.

There is a goal, and there is a process. Until we are able to do all the things we just read in the book of Job, we should not allow ourselves to get stuck or think we have arrived. How relevant is the Scripture that says deep calls unto deep (See Psalm 42:7). The darkness we see when we close our physical eyes is only the initiation. We must persist to go deeper into the depths of God until all we can perceive is light. There must once again be an illumination of everything that is presently cloaked in darkness, and man must arise again to assume the position given him initially when he was made in the image and likeness of God.

Arise, shine; for your light has come! And the glory of the Lord is risen upon you. For behold, the darkness shall cover the earth, and deep darkness the people; but the Lord will arise over you, and His glory will be seen upon you. The Gentiles shall come to your light, and kings to the brightness of your rising. "Lift up your eyes all around, and see: they all gather together, they come to you; your sons shall come from afar, and your daughters

shall be nursed at your side. Then you shall see and become radiant, and your heart shall swell with joy; because the abundance of the sea shall be turned to you, the wealth of the Gentiles shall come to you. The multitude of camels shall cover your land, the dromedaries of Midian and Ephah; all those from Sheba shall come; they shall bring gold and incense, and they shall proclaim the praises of the Lord. (Isaiah 60:1-6 - NKJV)

CONCLUSION

I dedicate this book to the next generation because I see something in them that gives me hope. If we can give them a proper foundation, then they can build a better world than we know now.

The immaturity of the human soul, particularly, the immaturity of believers is a problem for all of us. Remember, human beings are the most recent beings to grace creation, so we are the new kid on the block. Maturity is not something we acquire by faith but by going through the process. Similarly, a child goes through a process to transmute from infancy to adulthood. It is the same with our souls. It is born anew as a baby, but it must come into maturity for us to lay claim to original intent.

You may be tempted to think that what I am saying is not true because there are many who lay claim to maturity, who are, in fact, infants. There are characteristics that define maturity, and you can use these to judge yourself because only you, in the honesty of your own heart, can know where you stand on this journey. When you have mastered these within yourself, it will be easy for you to identify them in others, or the lack thereof.

Please note: There is an enemy within man who does not want the soul to come into maturity because it would mean the end of its existence: the ego. The ego is the false self in human beings that often parade around in the dark and camouflages its existence as god. I will share a little bit more about this once we look at the different characteristics of a maturing soul.

You Have Less Interest in Approval

The immature soul always seeks validation and approval from others. The mature soul is secured in him/herself, knowing who they are and to whom they belong. Getting the approval of others is not that important because the maturing soul lives for an audience of One: God.

You Process Issues Faster

The immature soul does not handle the turbulence of life very well. You constantly question, "Why me?" The maturing soul knows that issues are a part of the process and instead asks, "Why not me?"

The Ego Is Replaced by Equanimity

Equanimity is a sense of inner balance and poise in the emotional, mental, physical, and psychic levels. This is a stage of enlightenment; when the false self begins to die. This is where the ego gives the most resistance, and this is also the level where most people lose the battle towards maturation. The ego issues and beliefs are unveiled, processed, and released. This tends to lead to deeper processing, but peace and equanimity start to be revealed the deeper you go. The types of issues that people have to confront are varied. For those with a lot of pain to sift through, such as trauma or abuse, that peace may not come for some time, but it is there. Peace and inner equanimity have always been there. For the maturing soul, that is where they reside more. In turn, that makes you far less reactive to anything that is going on in the world. The drama of everyday life becomes of little interest and no cause for a reactive response to the maturing soul.

Deepening and Abiding Sense of Love

The maturing soul does not love in the sense of the romantic love that is hot and passionate and fervent. That kind of love is accessible to the maturing soul, but so are all the other kinds of love. Most important to a maturing soul is the love that embraces all as it is. That is true, unconditional love. As a person continues to mature, that is the love they abide in more and more in all situations. This abiding love is always here, just like that space of peace and equanimity. This points to the very human process of expanding and growing. Just like a tree growing in the woods, we seem to expand our hearts over time, filling up more and more of our lives.

You Are Drawn Towards Nourishment

Because a lot of the world's entertainment, activities, jobs, and relationships are very unhealthy, the maturing soul loses interest in a lot of these things. Many who are passing through stages of apathy are not really as apathetic as we may think. We are simply noticing what is unhealthy and are losing interest in it. That is not apathy. That is common sense. Anything that is not really nourishing, naturally becomes less and less of interest.

What is nourishing to a maturing soul becomes the primary focus. A maturing soul is drawn to nourishing relationships, places, work, and other things. The deepest nourishment, however, is always within, and that inner nourishment only makes it easier to see what is nourishing from the external world.

In this way, life simplifies for the maturing soul. Such a person looks at opportunities and asks after a fashion, "Does this nourish me or not?" It does not mean a maturing soul will not do difficult things; this person has already learned how discomfort and challenge can also feed their soul. But many difficulties and challenges are not necessary, and the maturing soul will flow towards wherever support and nourishment are most natural.

You Are At Ease in Letting Go

Another sign of a maturing soul is an ease in letting go. Nothing is ever lost. The maturing soul understands this. So if a job goes, then it goes. If a partnership is done, he/she lets that go. It does not mean they do not care. Quite the reverse; a maturing soul loves through letting go. Dragging something out that is over is painful, and the maturing soul is in no way interested in perpetuating suffering of any kind.

Furthermore, the maturing soul understands that when one thing leaves, space is made for another. The maturing soul is also at peace with remaining in this spaciousness without trying to fill it; patience is another hallmark of the maturing soul.

Sometimes life offers something to replace what has left. Sometimes, it does not. The maturing soul is not concerned either way. Only the ego cares about losing things, and the more mature the soul, the more at peace they are even when loved ones pass. They know that the soul is never separate from the divine; it only changes form.

You Appreciate the Human Process

We cannot bypass being human. Many traditions seem to be ignoring that we all go through phases and shifts and growth. In embracing the ultimate truth and divinity, this actually furthers our growth and impels us to face issues. We do not get away from ourselves. Maturing souls understand this. They do not look for the "ultimate" perfection of themselves. They understand that perfection is in Jesus alone. It is not an idea, and it can never be achieved as a form of doing.

Being is the ultimate realization, and with that space of being, the maturing soul naturally sheds layers of more and more subtle illusion and ego as they so choose and their path so determines. In this way, the maturing soul is at peace with however realized or unrealized they are, having the humility to dig deeper if they feel called and the self-love to accept themselves as they are.[8]

Now on the issue of the ego, let me share some final thoughts from a blog post I made prior to writing this book:

> *I will start this conversation, but I will leave it open for you to do your own research and draw your own conclusions.*
>
> *I held on to this revelation for a very good while because I was unsure of the timing of releasing it. But as I continued to observe the world, in tears, I have seen what Christianity has become. For me, it is a sad reality because as a student of the Word of God and having studied and followed some Christian mystics of our day, I know what Christianity can be. I am sure what it is predominantly now is not what Jesus intended when He established the church on His own broken body and spilled blood.*

---

[8]https://www.spiritualawakeningprocess.com/2015/05/signs-of-maturing-soul.html

> *We were given a tool to transform the world and usher in the manifested glory of God. Instead, we used it to serve our own whims and fantasies, to elevate ourselves to places of prominence and power, and made it about money. I finally know what is fundamentally wrong with Christianity. It is the ego we serve, thinking it is the true and living God. Which also suggest that the ego a.k.a. false self is a god of this world.*
>
> *I know Jesus dethroned the devil by His death, burial, resurrection and ascension so I have been trying to figure out who is this god of this world that blinds the minds of people to the truth. At first, I thought it was money because Jesus made a profound statement by claiming we cannot serve two masters; we cannot serve God and money. The love of money seems to be at the root of societies functionality so I thought mammon must definitely be the god of this world.*
>
> *Lo and behold, another god revealed itself just recently with the current trends.*
>
> *Now the ego is a false self, and it will not exist beyond our physical death. It is the ego that*

does not want to die; the ego that Paul referenced when he said, "I die daily." The ego is the "I" that interjects itself in areas of influence in our lives, often parading in the dark as the "voice of God," unbeknownst to us who follow its promptings blindly and without question.

The ego is of our own creation, which means its destruction must come by our own hands.

The ego demands to be right; it wants to be served and submitted to; obeyed and worshiped and given seats of prominence, special treatment, and always demands special recognition. Why is it so demanding, so hungry for attention? It does not want to die. In death, the ego ceases to exist, and it knows it has no eternal inheritance. It wants you to live so it can thrive and rule.

The whole purpose of going through difficulties and trauma is a process to try and dissolve the ego to destroy it and render it powerless.

The ego will keep us in fear as a survival mechanism. It does not want to be discovered, so it camouflages itself as God with Biblical

> *backing, but it does not want to die, for this is the only opportunity it gets at existing.*
>
> *For the soul to come into maturity, the ego must die. If the ego cannot die, it must be denied.*

I want to conclude this book by doing two things: firstly, I want to write a letter to my fourteen-year-old self (soul). I believe this will be helpful to a generation of teens who need to see themselves for more than they think they are. I do this for them because I wish someone had done it for me.

Finally, I want to share some additional Scriptures on the soul, with some annotations on some of these scriptures. This should aid in facilitating further study on the subject of man as a living soul.

As we have started this discussion on the soul, please dig deeply into this subject; Holy Spirit will help you. This knowledge of man as a living soul will be needed if we are ever going to become the full manifestation of God's original intention, both in heaven and on earth.

DEAR YOUNGER SOUL

I know at fourteen years old, you did not know a lot of things. You were grown up a bit sheltered and unexposed, only knowing the culture of community and church. So you know the quiet and good side of life. There was rarely any trauma in your life growing up, so you don't really know difficulty and hardship, outside of the occasional mouthing off at school and fights pushed that you showed no interest in. People thought you were weak and a coward, and maybe you were, but you managed to go through without getting into much trouble, so kudos.

There were many advancements made in the years leading up to your forty-fourth birthday that you were not privy to, and neither did it enter into your thoughts that these things were possible, and that is quite okay. I don't think we have a prophetic gift, per say, so not seeing the future may have prevented unnecessary burdens because you would not understand what you were looking at anyway. But never in my wildest dream did I think the world would change so much.

At fourteen, you did not know about cell phones or social media. There were no land phones, or maybe there was, but not for you. Communication was still by written letters and postal mail when distance was an issue. You had to see your friends to communicate with them, so it was more personal, enjoyable and less risky then to build relationships. You did not have access to a computer, internet, or a smart television, or any "smart" devices. None of these things seemed to exist in your world. Your parents did do a good thing when they sent you to computer class for those two summers. It was more about preventing you from being too idle than for you to learn the new technology being introduced to the world. I remember the lotus programs and having to type "WIN" at a DOS Prompt for windows to open up. There was a gateway with a black and white cow; I will never forget that. You still have those certificates in a file in the important drawer decades later. It is a reminder that you are not as dumb as you thought you were.

There are things I know now that I wish you knew then, and I thought I would write you since all human beings born in this world will pass by those teenage years, and maybe both of us can help them on their journey. I realize many young people like yourself are making worse choices than we made back then (they are exposed to a whole lot more too), and it is because they are incapable of seeing just how these choices frame the world that they and their children will experience tomorrow. There is no choice that doesn't sow a seed in the future that produces after its own kind, good or bad. It is also our power to choose that grows our soul into maturity, and this is vitality important, as I will mention later on.

At fourteen, you were still a virgin. You were yet to have your first girlfriend. As a matter of fact, you did not have a real girlfriend until your early twenties after going to a church camp. I think avoiding relationships was more out of fear or you just not being comfortable with your own body. You were a bit "fool fool" as well. You would not know what to do with a woman cause nobody taught you. You saw your father coming in drunk and beating your mother once. You saw your mom pull a knife on your father once. You saw a hardworking man going out every day to work, sometimes doing overtime, sometimes working on weekends. He worked hard, but you never really saw how a man treated a woman in terms of intimacy and emotions. So, when you did get a girlfriend, it was funny how that worked out. You didn't really know much about relationships, so it did not last as long as it could. You messed it up actually, out of sheer ignorance, and it is one regret you had to learn to live with. There is more to that story, but another time.

At fourteen, you didn't know much about the world. You left home to go to school, church, or shop. That was the sum total of your life. Occasionally your papa took you to a company function where you had delicacies like roast doctor fish and turtle soup. He also took you on a few trips to Salt River. Those were good but uncomfortable moments as you were inherently shy growing up. The only other trips I can remember is going to the country or visiting your aunt in Kingston. People have more adventurous stories to tell about their teenage years, but not you.

You did have fun in the community with the guys from the community. You played football, cricket outside your gate, build bush homes outside, played in the rain, sailed paper boats on the running water after a good shower of rain, climb trees, ran out in the streets with your little brother wearing only your underwear while it rained, and created forms and figures from mud. You used a makeshift noose made from coconut leaves to catch lizards, dropped big rocks on frogs, chased white chickens back into their coup when the sun went down, avoided scorpion bites, were bitten several times by wasp all over your face, and almost lost an eye to a jealous cock and trying to play hide and seek in a drum of water. Now that I look back, it all sounds like fun --- fun the generations after you and going forward is not familiar with. Compared to your life, I think this generation of teenagers is boring. All they do is spend time on tablets and phones, and if the WIFI ever stops working, they begin to lose their minds. Yes, WIFI (internet) is a big necessity now, or the world would stop moving or maybe cease to exist, it seems. I don't even know what WIFI means, but google knows. Yes, Google knows everything about everything; so constant library visits and perusing pages of the Brittanica Enclyclopias are a distant thing of the past.

The emergence of smart technology has changed the world and how we interact with each other. If you took a walk in the airport now, you would notice that no one is looking at anyone much. From the toddler to the adult, everyone has their eyes buried in either a phone or a tablet. It is weird because the face to face interaction humanity once knew is waning into nothingness or non-existence. It becomes challenging to meet new friends or connect with strangers. No one seems interested in that anymore. At least, not offline.

Yes, the world is very different now than it was when you were fourteen --- very different. You would not believe how much change can happen in thirty years, so I figured the next thirty years will be substantially different as well.

So let me tell you about the age that we are now in. In addition to what I have already mentioned, the world is experiencing a global pandemic as we speak that has caused countries globally to literally lockdown. Borders have been closed to sea and air travel on occasions, and many restrictions have been implemented, including mandatory mask wearing, social distancing (3-6 feet apart), and increased personal hygiene. Schools closed down for months, then began to implement online learning through platforms like zoom and google classrooms. Some teachers had to resort to what is known as WhatsApp, which is a phone messaging service owned by Facebook and used by almost everyone who has a phone. Churches also closed down, but most governments allowed them to open up as long as they adhered to the protocols in place, because what is a society without a praying church. I am yet to see how effective our prayer is because one thing to note: while the world changed, the church has seemingly remained the same (we still sing the same songs they did when you were going---read the same scriptures---preach the same messages---pretty much, everything is the same), which really brings me to the meat of the matter.

The church (body of Christ) had a greater responsibility than we have actually lived out for centuries. We were supposed to be the pioneers of new technologies released from heaven, leaders in our own rights, having positions in influential spheres of society, that is, political, scientific, technology, medicine; instead, we were sold a doctrine to believe Jesus was coming any minute now that literally immobilize us from becoming active pursuers of excellence and positions of influence and change. We sat in church week after week, trying to get non-Christians to jump on board because the world was going to end; so, sadly, the world changed, but we did not.

Unfortunately, this mentality was sold to you at a very young age, causing you to have no interest in healthy living, academic excellence, or becoming an agent of change in society. What would be the point if the

The Soul of Man

world was ending anyway? On top of that, you were told very negative things that accompanied a bad report card that caused you to believe you were dumb, good for nothing and not worth the earth you were walking on. That was also the doctrine of the church; how unworthy we are: wretches, bastards, the scum of the earth, no good, etc. Which essentially meant that your belief system was predominantly "God was in love with a piece of trash." Most people who grew up in the church lacked self-esteem and self-value. There was also no motivation because all we saw in the future was doom, destruction, and the end of the world. Subsequently, having this mindset meant you didn't dream big or aspired to become much. You had no idea just how valuable and powerful you are because nobody told you. Life was about surviving and being ready for Jesus' return. You did not believe for a second that you would see your thirtieth birthday, so when you did, it felt like it just crept up on you unawares. Suddenly, you were thirty-five and getting married. The shock and unpreparedness developed anxiety in your heart. Life was moving pretty fast all of a sudden, and you were getting old. Before you knew it, you were celebrating your forty-fourth birthday, which is the year this book was written and published.

Before you became the prominent writer, speaker, and publisher with little to no academic qualifications (I'm really tooting your horn here), you were a supermarket attendant, sander, mattress maker, construction worker, and a surveying draughtsman. You worked with a drunk, a narcissist, an adulterer, and two money-lovers who showed no interest in sharing their wealth with those who worked for them. By God's grace, you were able to start two online companies: one where you wrote and sold thousands of copies of your plays and skits to a global market. You had some help to get this off the ground, but once you did, it was your ticket out of the nine-to-five environment. This also led to a spin-off company where you offered writing and self-publishing service to clients all over the world. You did well for yourself, considering the circumstances, but you had the potential for so much more, but you did not learn this until well in your thirties or early forties. No one taught you what it truly means to be human; that nothing is really impossible. Yes, you heard it at church, but not many people lived it out as an example. People took loans to buy cars, a mortgage to buy houses, and student loans (with a ridiculously high interest rate) to go to school. The God who parted Red Seas and healed people and raised people from the dead was not a living example in your life.

Knowing what I know now, I would tell you to take school seriously; to beg your parents to help you go to college, and get a career that would help humanity, not something that is popular, with the highest hiring rate and potential to make more money. Money is not as important as what money can do.

So, my fourteen-year-old soul, stay in church but question everything. Learn to think for yourself, study for yourself and draw your own conclusions of life and truth. Ask God to help you and trust the help He sends.

That spiritual being who sat on your bed during your darkest days was not a demon. You kept your eyes closed and wished it would leave; it was sent to help you, but you had no idea how to engage with the unseen world. You were actually taught that anything spiritual was a demon, so when a presence walked into a room, and the hair on your body stood up, you automatically thought it was a demon. It was not. The God you knew then was full of wrath, judgmental, unloving, and quick to send people to hell for the simplest of things, for example, body piercings, tattoos, missing church, and being inappropriately dressed.

Here is a Scripture I would want you to pay special attention to:

But you have come to Mount Zion and to the city of the living God, the heavenly Jerusalem, to an innumerable company of angels, to the general assembly and church of the firstborn who are registered in heaven, to God the Judge of all, to the spirits of just men made perfect, to Jesus the Mediator of the new covenant, and to the blood of sprinkling that speaks better things than that of Abel. (Hebrews 12:22-24 - NKJV).

This is the Glorious Company in which you have found yourself. Learn to engage with it. God will help you. By the way, the God you met in your thirties was very different from the "church god." He is far more relatable, loving, compassionate, and has a vested interest in even the smallest detail of your life. I wish you knew Him then. His goal is not to end the world but to save it, and He wants to do it in partnership with you.

So, the world is not coming to an end. As a matter of fact, your chosen religion will try to convince you that Christianity is about getting into heaven; it is not. The moment you say yes to Jesus, you are already there.

And raised us up together, and made us sit together in the heavenly places in Christ Jesus. (Ephesians 2:6 - NKJV)

You are there, seated with Christ in heavenly places. Your duty is to learn how to live from there to here because you were actually sent here for a purpose. Yes, you existed in heaven in spirit form, in the mind of God before you came here, which means before getting saved at seventeen, you were counted among God's prodigal sons. You needed to find your way home, and you did; you just never quite grasp what that truly meant, so it took you a while to come into the things I am sharing with you now.

You struggle with prayer all your Christian life. It's not because you did not want to pray, but you have always desired authenticity, so when it seemed like prayer was just you talking to the wind, your mind would not let you pray. You tried everything, every book, every practice, every advice to try to get into the habit of prayer, but to little avail. You do talk to God heart to heart; you do maintain somewhat of a connection within; you do sometimes pray when asked at church (though uncomfortable as it is); but you struggle with this thing, my young soul.

Here is a good prayer to get into the habit of praying:

> **Our Father in heaven,**
> **Hallowed be Your name.**
> **Your kingdom come.**
> **Your will be done**
> **On earth as it is in heaven.**
> **Give us this day our daily bread.**
> **And forgive us our debts,**
> **As we forgive our debtors.**
> **And do not lead us into temptation,**
> **But deliver us from the evil one.**
> **For Yours is the kingdom and the power**
> **and the glory forever. Amen.**
> **(Matthew 6:9-13 - NKJV).**

You struggled with making a daily habit out of reading the Bible. You eventually got acclimated to it way up in your twenties, and it did wonders for you. You started to teach and preach at church, took on leadership roles, etc. I was amazed at what reading the Bible from cover to cover did, but then you should have continued reading, but you stopped. I encourage you to make it a habit to read through the Bible every year, and read different translations. You don't have to understand what you read, so don't pause too much trying to figure it out. Just read. Your new soul is far more intellectual and able to absorb high levels of communication/information and mystery than you realize. Your duty is to just read. Just read.

At some point in your life, you will notice that there is a disparity between the Biblical narrative and your life. It is going to throw you into a quandary because you believe your life pursuing God should read like the Biblical text, but it doesn't. It is way different, but is it really! You eventually spent time studying Genesis 1-3 and realize that in our fallen state, the presence of God, and God Himself, still pursues us. We are the ones hiding and trying to cover ourselves. So heaven interacts with us daily, and it has nothing to do with qualifying for God's visitation. Every human being is automatically qualified for God to visit them, and He does --- well, at least the host of heaven does.

Life is very interesting, if you learn to hear and see. It is not about what you see with your physical eyes either --- it goes much deeper than that. The ignorance of the previous generations may have shut down our capacity to see as children because we played with imaginary friends, and saw things that they could not see. There were beings that woke my mother up when I was crying as a baby. My father had his own set of stories to tell, but for them, it was all demons. For some reason, Christians demonized the spiritual realm, and the only thing they accepted from the Spirit was tongues and shaking uncontrollably. So we were taught to shut out the spiritual dimension to our own detriment. It became an uphill journey to regain access with the clarity I believe we should have. But I know you are depending on me to do it, so I will not give up. When you get to my age, the world must be better than it is now, and it is our duty and responsibility to make it happen.

From an older soul to a younger soul, one of the most vital pieces of information I can pass on to you is the need to mature your soul. As an unbeliever, with a soul that is devoid of life, if you can mature your soul, you can accomplish great feats, as history has demonstrated repeatedly. Imagine the unlimited potential for the believer who learns how to mature their souls. The idea that all things are possible only makes sense to the one who has a matured soul, whether you are a believer or not. This is access given to humanity.

Do not practice to look at the world through a divided lens. There is one humanity. In the beginning God made man, not Christians and non-Christians, not black and white, not rich and poor. Every human being has a divine spark. If that light is completely vanquished, such a one will dwell in darkness. You are light, and light dispels darkness by virtue of its presence. Without doing anything other than showing up, your light begins to illuminate your environment. There is no darkness that light cannot penetrate.

Young soul, never underestimate the power of you showing up in every place your feet will take you because you are an embodiment of divinity.

Pay attention to your speech and thoughts. They create your future and the reality and experiences you have. Paul understood this very well when he said:

Finally, brethren, whatever things are true, whatever things are noble, whatever things are just, whatever things are pure, whatever things are lovely, whatever things are of good report, if there is any virtue and if there is anything praiseworthy—meditate on these things. (Philippians 4:8 - NKJV).

Life is difficult, but if you focus on the negative stuff, it will multiply. Whatever you gaze at, multiplies. That is a spiritual principle no one taught you growing up. It is important how you see, how you hear, and how you think.

You are not a failure.

You are not a loser.

You were not born to suffer.

You are unique – one of a kind – a gem in the Father's eyes.

You are important to God.

You and God have an agreement for you to come to earth and accomplish a purpose. There is a divine destiny embedded in your very existence.

You were not a mistake. You are here because you are supposed to be here. You wanted to be here. You wanted to come to earth to accomplish the Father's will. You wanted to do great things to bring glory and honour to His name.

It doesn't matter what people think about you. Consider their thoughts and what they say as reference only. Learn to absorb what is good and beneficial and discard the rest like the garbage that it is.

God's eyes are always on you. His presence is always with you. You are in a great and glorious company.

Even saints who have already passed on are aligning with you so you can accomplish your purpose, and if there is time, you may be called upon to also finish that which another started. Live in a constant awareness that God is with you. Live in the consciousness that you are surrounded by a glorious company of heavenly hosts.

You are one, but you represent a majority. Your life will count for many generations to come because the world you make today, is the world the next generation will live in tomorrow.

You hold the keys to unlock the possibilities embedded in humanity by first unlocking that which is within you. Focus on you. Change you. Fix you. Creation is waiting on you to emerge, not on what you do.

Your gifts and talents are as unique as your DNA and fingerprint. No one can do what you do; no one can be you.

Your voice is known in heaven; it is known in creation. What you say has divine value, so think God-thoughts and speak as if God is speaking through you.

You are light.

You are a life-giver. The living water resides in you, so let it flow. Be a river and not a lake. Keep moving, keep growing, keep learning, and you will grow your soul into the divine entity that it was meant to be.

Approach every difficult situation and people with a smile on your face; trials come to make you strong. Every negative circumstance can be transmuted by gratitude and acceptance. It will unlock greater glory within you and make you stronger.

You are more than a conqueror. You don't just walk away in victory, but you walk away stronger than you were before. Every challenge and obstacle in your life was meant to be overcome.

I believe in you, young soul; I believe in your potential to change this world, and you will.

Shalom (Peace).

It is well!

ADDITIONAL TEXT ON THE SOUL

There are 498 references to the "Soul" in the King James Version (KJV). These are just a few of them:

Genesis 2:7

And the Lord God formed man of the dust of the ground, and breathed into his nostrils the breath of life; and man became a living soul.

Genesis 12:5

And Abram took Sarai his wife, and Lot his brother's son, and all their substance that they had gathered, and the souls that they had gotten in Haran; and they went forth to go into the land of Canaan; and into the land of Canaan they came.

Genesis 35:18

And it came to pass, as her soul was in departing, (for she died) that she called his name Benoni: but his father called him Benjamin.

Exodus 30:16

And thou shalt take the atonement money of the children of Israel, and shalt appoint it for the service of the tabernacle of the congregation; that it may be a memorial unto the children of Israel before the Lord, to make an atonement for your souls.

Leviticus 4:2

Speak unto the children of Israel, saying, If a soul shall sin through ignorance against any of the commandments of the Lord concerning things which ought not to be done, and shall do against any of them.

Leviticus 5:1

And if a soul sin, and hear the voice of swearing, and is a witness, whether he hath seen or known of it; if he do not utter it, then he shall bear his iniquity.

Leviticus 5:17

And if a soul sin, and commit any of these things which are forbidden to be done by the commandments of the Lord; though he wist it not, yet is he guilty, and shall bear his iniquity.

Leviticus 17:11

For the life of the flesh is in the blood: and I have given it to you upon the altar to make an atonement for your souls: for it is the blood that maketh an atonement for the soul.

Numbers 31:50

We have therefore brought an oblation for the Lord, what every man hath gotten, of jewels of gold, chains, and bracelets, rings, earrings, and tablets, to make an atonement for our souls before the Lord.

Deuteronomy 4:29

But if from thence thou shalt seek the Lord thy God, thou shalt find him, if thou seek him with all thy heart and with all thy soul.

Deuteronomy 6:5

And thou shalt love the Lord thy God with all thine heart, and with all thy soul, and with all thy might.

Deuteronomy 11:13

And it shall come to pass, if ye shall hearken diligently unto my commandments which I command you this day, to love the Lord your God, and to serve him with all your heart and with all your soul.

Deuteronomy 11:18

Therefore shall ye lay up these my words in your heart and in your soul, and bind them for a sign upon your hand, that they may be as frontlets between your eyes.

1 Samuel 18:1

And it came to pass, when he had made an end of speaking unto Saul, that the soul of Jonathan was knit with the soul of David, and Jonathan loved him as his own soul.

1 Kings 17:21

And he stretched himself upon the child three times, and cried unto the Lord, and said, O Lord my God, I pray thee, let this child's soul come into him again.

1 Kings 17:22

And the Lord heard the voice of Elijah; and the soul of the child came into him again, and he revived.

Job 12:10

In whose hand is the soul of every living thing, and the breath of all mankind.

Job 33:30

To bring back his soul from the pit, to be enlightened with the light of the living.

Psalm 16:10

For thou wilt not leave my soul in hell; neither wilt thou suffer thine Holy One to see corruption.

Psalm 23:3

He restoreth my soul: he leadeth me in the paths of righteousness for his name's sake.

Psalm 26:9

Gather not my soul with sinners, nor my life with bloody men.

Psalm 30:3

O Lord, thou hast brought up my soul from the grave: thou hast kept me alive, that I should not go down to the pit.

Psalm 42:1

As the hart panteth after the water brooks, so panteth my soul after thee, O God.

Psalm 42:2

My soul thirsteth for God, for the living God: when shall I come and appear before God?

Psalm 56:13

For thou hast delivered my soul from death: wilt not thou deliver my feet from falling, that I may walk before God in the light of the living?

Psalm 107:9

For he satisfieth the longing soul, and filleth the hungry soul with goodness.

Psalm 107:26

They mount up to the heaven, they go down again to the depths: their soul is melted because of trouble.

Psalm 121:7

The Lord shall preserve thee from all evil: he shall preserve thy soul.

Psalm 139:14

I will praise thee; for I am fearfully and wonderfully made: marvellous are thy works; and that my soul knoweth right well.

Proverbs 2:10

When wisdom entereth into thine heart, and knowledge is pleasant unto thy soul.

(The soul appreciates knowledge. It desires to learn that which it does not yet know.)

Proverbs 6:32

But whoso committeth adultery with a woman lacketh understanding: he that doeth it destroyeth his own soul.

Proverbs 8:36

But he that sinneth against me wrongeth his own soul: all they that hate me love death.

Proverbs 11:30

The fruit of the righteous is a tree of life; and he that winneth souls is wise.

Proverbs 15:32

He that refuseth instruction despiseth his own soul: but he that heareth reproof getteth understanding.

Proverbs 16:17

The highway of the upright is to depart from evil: he that keepeth his way preserveth his soul.

Proverbs 19:2

Also, that the soul be without knowledge, it is not good; and he that hasteth with his feet sinneth.

Proverbs 19:8

He that getteth wisdom loveth his own soul: he that keepeth understanding shall find good.

Isaiah 1:14

Your new moons and your appointed feasts my soul hateth: they are a trouble unto me; I am weary to bear them.

(Does God have a soul?).

Isaiah 10:18

And shall consume the glory of his forest, and of his fruitful field, both soul and body: and they shall be as when a standard-bearer fainteth.

(There is no mention of the spirit of man).

Isaiah 26:9

With my soul have I desired thee in the night; yea, with my spirit within me will I seek thee early: for when thy judgments are in the earth, the inhabitants of the world will learn righteousness.

(The spirit within is mentioned here).

Isaiah 42:1

Behold my servant, whom I uphold; mine elect, in whom my soul delighteth; I have put my spirit upon him: he shall bring forth judgment to the Gentiles.

Isaiah 53:10

Yet it pleased the Lord to bruise him; he hath put him to grief: when thou shalt make his soul an offering for sin, he shall see his seed, he shall prolong his days, and the pleasure of the Lord shall prosper in his hand.

Isaiah 53:12

Therefore will I divide him a portion with the great, and he shall divide the spoil with the strong; because he hath poured out his soul unto death: and he was numbered with the transgressors;

and he bare the sin of many, and made intercession for the transgressors.

Isaiah 57:16

For I will not contend for ever, neither will I be always wroth: for the spirit should fail before me, and the souls which I have made.

Isaiah 61:10

I will greatly rejoice in the Lord, my soul shall be joyful in my God; for he hath clothed me with the garments of salvation, he hath covered me with the robe of righteousness, as a bridegroom decketh himself with ornaments, and as a bride adorneth herself with her jewels.

(There are two garments of the soul listed here).

Jeremiah 5:9

Shall I not visit for these things? saith the Lord: and shall not my soul be avenged on such a nation as this?

(Again, does God have a soul?).

Jeremiah 6:8

Be thou instructed, O Jerusalem, lest my soul depart from thee; lest I make thee desolate, a land not inhabited.

Jeremiah 6:16

Thus saith the Lord, Stand ye in the ways, and see, and ask for the old paths, where is the good way, and walk therein, and ye shall find rest for your souls. But they said, We will not walk therein.

(Finding the ancient paths)

Jeremiah 38:16

So Zedekiah the king sware secretly unto Jeremiah, saying, As the Lord liveth, that made us this soul, I will not put thee to death, neither will I give thee into the hand of these men that seek thy life.

Ezekiel 4:14

Then said I, Ah Lord God! behold, my soul hath not been polluted: for from my youth up even till now have I not eaten of that which dieth of itself, or is torn in pieces; neither came there abominable flesh into my mouth.

(The soul can be polluted).

Ezekiel 13:18

And say, Thus saith the Lord God; Woe to the women that sew pillows to all armholes, and make kerchiefs upon the head of every stature to hunt souls! Will ye hunt the souls of my people, and will ye save the souls alive that come unto you?

Ezekiel 18:4

Behold, all souls are mine; as the soul of the father, so also the soul of the son is mine: the soul that sinneth, it shall die.

Ezekiel 18:20

The soul that sinneth, it shall die. The son shall not bear the iniquity of the father, neither shall the father bear the iniquity of the son: the righteousness of the righteous shall be upon him, and the wickedness of the wicked shall be upon him.

Habakkuk 2:10

Thou hast consulted shame to thy house by cutting off many people, and hast sinned against thy soul.

Matthew 10:28

And fear not them which kill the body, but are not able to kill the soul: but rather fear him which is able to destroy both soul and body in hell.

(The soul can be destroyed by the One who made it!)

The Soul of Man

Matthew 12:18

Behold my servant, whom I have chosen; my beloved, in whom my soul is well pleased: I will put my spirit upon him, and he shall shew judgment to the Gentiles.

Matthew 16:26

For what is a man profited, if he shall gain the whole world, and lose his own soul? or what shall a man give in exchange for his soul?

(Is there anything that has a greater value than the soul?)

Matthew 22:37

Jesus said unto him, Thou shalt love the Lord thy God with all thy heart, and with all thy soul, and with all thy mind.

Mark 8:37

Or what shall a man give in exchange for his soul?

Mark 12:33

And to love him with all the heart, and with all the understanding, and with all the soul, and with all the strength, and to love his neighbour as himself, is more than all whole burnt offerings and sacrifices.

Luke 2:35

(Yea, a sword shall pierce through thy own soul also,) that the thoughts of many hearts may be revealed.

Luke 21:19

In your patience possess ye your souls.

Acts 2:27

Because thou wilt not leave my soul in hell, neither wilt thou suffer thine Holy One to see corruption.

Acts 2:31

He seeing this before spake of the resurrection of Christ, that his soul was not left in hell, neither his flesh did see corruption.

Acts 2:41

Then they that gladly received his word were baptized: and the same day there were added unto them about three thousand souls.

Acts 4:32

And the multitude of them that believed were of one heart and of one soul: neither said any of them that ought of the things which he possessed was his own; but they had all things common.

Acts 14:22

Confirming the souls of the disciples, and exhorting them to continue in the faith, and that we must through much tribulation enter into the kingdom of God.

Romans 2:9

Tribulation and anguish, upon every soul of man that doeth evil, of the Jew first, and also of the Gentile.

(Why the emphasis on the soul?)

1 Corinthians 15:45

And so it is written, The first man Adam was made a living soul; the last Adam was made a quickening spirit.

2 Corinthians 1:23

Moreover I call God for a record upon my soul, that to spare you I came not as yet unto Corinth.

(There is a Godly record on the soul!)

1 Thessalonians 5:23

And the very God of peace sanctify you wholly; and I pray God your whole spirit and soul and body be preserved blameless unto the coming of our Lord Jesus Christ.

The Soul of Man

(This is the only text of scripture with body, soul, and spirit in the same sentence).

Hebrews 4:12

For the word of God is quick, and powerful, and sharper than any twoedged sword, piercing even to the dividing asunder of soul and spirit, and of the joints and marrow, and is a discerner of the thoughts and intents of the heart.

Hebrews 6:19

Which hope we have as an anchor of the soul, both sure and stedfast, and which entereth into that within the veil.

(Hope is an anchor for the soul.)

Hebrews 10:39

But we are not of them who draw back unto perdition; but of them that believe to the saving of the soul.

Hebrews 13:17

Obey them that have the rule over you, and submit yourselves: for they watch for your souls, as they must give account, that they may do it with joy, and not with grief: for that is unprofitable for you.

James 1:21

Wherefore lay apart all filthiness and superfluity of naughtiness, and receive with meekness the engrafted word, which is able to save your souls.

James 5:20

Let him know, that he which converteth the sinner from the error of his way shall save a soul from death, and shall hide a multitude of sins.

1 Peter 1:9

Receiving the end of your faith, even the salvation of your souls.

1 Peter 1:22

Seeing ye have purified your souls in obeying the truth through the Spirit unto unfeigned love of the brethren, see that ye love one another with a pure heart fervently:

1 Peter 2:11

Dearly beloved, I beseech you as strangers and pilgrims, abstain from fleshly lusts, which war against the soul.

1 Peter 2:25

For ye were as sheep going astray; but are now returned unto the Shepherd and Bishop of your souls.

3 John 1:2

Beloved, I wish above all things that thou mayest prosper and be in health, even as thy soul prospereth.

Revelation 6:9

And when he had opened the fifth seal, I saw under the altar the souls of them that were slain for the word of God, and for the testimony which they held.

Revelation 16:3

And the second angel poured out his vial upon the sea; and it became as the blood of a dead man: and every living soul died in the sea.

Revelation 18:13

And cinnamon, and odours, and ointments, and frankincense, and wine, and oil, and fine flour, and wheat, and beasts, and sheep, and horses, and chariots, and slaves, and souls of men.

Revelation 20:4

And I saw thrones, and they sat upon them, and judgment was given unto them: and I saw the souls of them that were beheaded for the witness of Jesus, and for the word of God, and which had not worshipped the beast, neither his image, neither had received his mark upon their foreheads, or in their hands;

and they lived and reigned with Christ a thousand years.

QUOTES FOR THE MATURING SOUL

Release all your attachment to your agendas. Your soul knows better. It won't trip. Trust your soul's wisdom. You have the answers to your questions.

Anything is possible, if you've got enough nerve.

Change is inevitable, but transformation is by conscious choice.

When you replace "Why is this happening to me" with "What is this trying to teach me?", everything shifts.

When we strive to become better than we are, everything around us becomes better too.

You are the greatest project you will ever get to work on. Take your time. Create magic.

And like the moon, we must go through phases of emptiness to feel full again.

When you heal, you will understand why you broke.

My biggest enemy is myself, my inner darkness. My biggest strength can be that darkness. It can't be defeated because it is a part of me. I can only transform it to something useful.

Become aware of the silent but powerful sense of God's presence.

Use every breathe to allow the awareness of God to grow deeper.

Fill yourself up with so much love, light, joy, and gratitude that you cannot help but raise the vibration of everyone you encounter.

You cannot win in life if you are losing in your mind. Change your thoughts, and it will change your life.

- *Tony Gaskins*

Everything that happens to you is your teacher. The secret is to learn to sit at the feet of your own life and be taught by it.

Everything that has happened to you is either an opportunity to grow or an obstacle to prevent you from growing --- you get to choose.

- *Wayne Dyer*

Know the difference between those who feed your ego and those who feed your soul.

I am remembering who I am, and why I came here.

Of the thousand million children competing for fertilization, it was you, only you, that emerged. To distill so specific a form from that chaos of improbability, like turning air to gold, that is the crowning unlikelihood. The thermodynamic miracle.

C. Orville McLeish

- *Dr. Manhattan*

Something will grow from all you are going through. And it will be you.

www.ingramcontent.com/pod-product-compliance
Lightning Source LLC
Chambersburg PA
CBHW071454070526
44578CB00001B/331